NOBODY SAYS "PLEASE" IN THE PSALMS

Patricia Gits Opatz

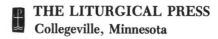

THE LITURGICAL PRESS
Collegeville, Minnesota

Nihil obstat: Robert C. Harren, J.C.L., *Censor deputatus.*

Imprimatur: ✝ George H. Speltz, D.D., Bishop of St. Cloud, Minnesota. November 22, 1983.

Cover design by Mary Jo Pauly.

2	3	4	5	6	7	8

Printed in the United States of America.
ISBN 0-8146-1326-8

For my husband Ralph

Contents

Introduction

The title for this book was created quite spontaneously during a class I was team-teaching with Fr. Daniel Durken, O.S.B. In commenting on certain passages from the Gospel of Luke, I pointed out that Jesus uses very plain and direct language in the Lord's Prayer. He does not say, "Please, Father, we beseech you vouchsafe to give us this day our daily bread, if it be your holy will." His request is simple, almost a command: "Give us this day our daily bread." I observed how similarly the psalms are worded—they are direct, frank, even blunt—and I commented, "Nobody says 'please' in the psalms."

The title fits because this little book is about the psalms as prayers which were designed by God for all of us to use. He put a powerful weapon in our hands when he gave us the psalms, for they enable us to say things to God which we might not

otherwise have the nerve to say. In these prayers
we have God's permission to speak to him inti-
mately and boldly, to show our joy, love and trust
as well as our fear, anger, anxiety, and frustration. No other prayer book dares encourage such
an intimate relationship with God as does the Book
of Psalms. What a comfort to know that the
mighty Creator and Lord of the universe desires
close familiar conversation with each one of us
and has kindly provided the words for us to
use—words to chide, to complain, to question, and
to plead as well as words to love.

The psalms are the prayers of real people living through human dilemmas and predicaments
not basically different from what we face today.
Psalm writers too had their hills and valleys, their
highs and lows, and they took them all to God in
prayer just as we do. Because these psalms are
divinely inspired, the work of the Holy Spirit,
when we discover in them certain attitudes,
points of view, emotions, and outbursts, we can
feel safe in adopting these for our own use. That is
what God intended—that we should use this
prayer book for our needs just as the Jews did, as
Jesus, Mary and Joseph did, as the apostles did.
This old book is one of those precious family heir-
looms passed down through the generations, not
to be wrapped in tissue and stored away, but to be
used and then handed on. And now it's our turn.

The six chapters in this book develop attitudes
found in the psalmist's prayer which we could use

in our own: frankness, trust, praise, love for God's dwelling place, dealing with dry times in prayer, and coping with sin. Following each chapter are questions which may be used for private reflection or for group discussion.

I hope this small book will encourage readers not only to turn to the psalms frequently when they pray, but also to take the mind of the psalmist into all their prayers and into their lives— just as Jesus did.

1

Frankly Speaking

It's a charming scene: the young man decides to tell his sweetheart he loves her dearly, she is the only one for him, and he wants to marry her. He arranges a meeting with her and, to the background strains of romantic music, begins to declare his love. Taking a booklet from his pocket, he reads aloud tender speeches of love made by other men to other women at other times. Because some of them use stilted language and archaic words, they do not sound like the young man at all. He hardly glances at her, but keeps reading as if it were very important to get it all in before he stops. How does this woman feel? Wouldn't most women begin to wonder? "Why is he reading these words instead of saying what is in his heart? Can't he find words of his own? How can he remain so distant and formal? And he scarcely looks at me. Does he really care about me?"

Unfortunately, this is a picture of the way some of us treat God in those times we set aside for conversation with him. Instead of using our own words to say what is in our hearts, we rely on the words and thoughts of others, frequently in language which does not sound like us at all. And yet God is not really content with such a distant, formal relationship. Scripture makes it plain that he is a lover, a friend, a member of the family —and we should speak to him as if we believe that.

There is a time for using formal prepared prayers, of course. Certainly in public liturgical prayer such forms are indispensable. And even in our private prayer we sometimes find it helpful to use words that other friends of God have composed. The psalms, in particular, are the prayers of others, inspired by God, which we can find so practical and meaningful in our own lives.

If we pray the psalms faithfully over a period of time, though, we will surely discover the psalmist doing what we perhaps should do more: speaking to God very frankly and openly. Theirs is obviously an intimate relationship, and the writer of the psalms apparently feels comfortable being open and even bold with God; at no time does he stand on ceremony. In fact, at times he is surprisingly audacious. No matter what his mood, what trouble he is suffering, or what joy he is celebrating, he shares it all, confident that the Lord will listen and care.

Speaking to God as if he were speaking to a close friend, the psalmist freely expresses very human emotions. In Psalm 9, for example, he calls the Lord "a stronghold in distress" (v. 10); yet in the very next psalm, he challenges God, "Why do you hide in times of distress?" (Ps 10:1). Haven't we all known such abrupt changes in our attitude toward God? But do we feel as comfortable as the psalmist telling God about them?

The psalmist sometimes uses daring ways of putting pressure on God to help him. One such way is to remind God that he will be of no use if he is dead. In Psalm 6, we see one of his reminders:

> For among the dead no one remembers you;
> In the nether world who gives you thanks? (v. 6).

Again in Psalm 30 he questions God:

> What gain would there be from my lifeblood,
>   from my going down into the grave?
> Would dust give you thanks
>   or proclaim your faithfulness? (v. 10).

Clearly he is telling God that he is of more good to him alive than dead. He can thank and praise God, but his dust cannot, so God should—if he is at all sensible—spare the psalmist's life. It may sound foolish from a strictly rational point of view, but it is a heartfelt prayer and apparently quite acceptable to God.

The psalmist uses a similar device when he says, in effect, "If you don't save me now, it is going to make you look very bad!" This will happen because his enemies will triumph and exult over him, knowing full well he had been trusting in God to help him. (See Ps 13:4-6.) Psalm 79 also pleads for God's help "because of the glory of your name." The speaker asks for pardon and help so that his enemies cannot taunt him by asking, "Where is your God?" (vv. 9-10).

Many a twentieth-century Christian can identify with the psalmist's feeling that God is being mocked and might also feel inclined to pray:

> Grant me a proof of your favor,
>> that my enemies may see, to their confusion,
>> that you, O Lord, have helped and comforted me.
>>> (Ps 86:17)

It is a daring prayer, not very likely found in any prayer book except the psalms. Who but God would take such a familiar approach?

The speaker in the psalms even feels comfortable pointing out that God should help him because—well, he deserves it; he has been innocent and faithful. Could we pray that way, I wonder, or would we feel irreverent and presumptuous? Psalm 17 is just one example of such a fearless prayer:

> Though you test my heart, searching it in the night,
>> though you try me with fire, you shall find no
>> malice in me.
> My mouth has not transgressed after the manner
>> of man;
>> according to the words of your lips I have kept
>> the ways of the law (vv. 3-4).

In Psalm 26, too, the psalmist pleads that he has kept his integrity, never wavering in his trust. Confident that he will be found innocent, he invites God to search his heart and soul. Most of us might be afraid of praying so boldly, fearful of sounding like the hypocritical Pharisee in the temple, but the psalmist honestly expresses his feelings.

To be sure, there are the penitential psalms too (e.g., Pss 6, 32, 38, 51), in which the speaker, rather than pointing out his fidelity, admits that he has sinned, repents, and asks God's forgiveness. But whether he is protesting his innocence or confessing his guilt, he is open and uninhibited before God.

Nor does the psalmist hesitate to tell God to "Hurry up!" Such an imperative is included frequently in his prayers: "Make haste to help me," he cries repeatedly (Pss 40:14; 69:18; 70:2, 6). Sometimes in his anguish he becomes even more impassioned: "Awake! Why are you asleep, O Lord?" (Ps 44:24).

In all these situations we can see the psalms are very personal prayers, spoken spontaneously from the heart. Confident that God hears and cares, the speaker frankly shares the deepest anguish, the worst fears, and the loftiest joys with this God who has made himself so available.

There are other men and women in Scripture who demonstrate this same intimacy with God which we might try to imitate. Consider the conversation in which Abraham bargains with God to spare the city of Sodom, which is destined for destruction because of its sins. There is a beautiful blend of boldness and deference as Abraham states his case. Respectfully he prefaces one argument, "See how I am presuming to speak to my Lord, though I am but dust and ashes." In another place, pressing his case, he apologizes, "Let not my Lord grow impatient if I go on." But go on he does. It is almost as if he is trying to shame God: "Far be it from you to do such a thing, to make the innocent die with the guilty. Should not the judge of all the world act with justice?" (Gen 18:22-32).

God accepts Abraham's repeated arguments and is not angered by Abraham's persistence. Obviously Abraham does not underestimate God as we so often do, nor does he think of God as remote and unapproachable.

The same combination of reverence and familiarity is found in Jeremiah. Dismayed to observe how often evil people live in prosperity and contentment, Jeremiah speaks to God: "You would be in the right, O Lord, if I should dispute with you; even so, I must discuss the case with you" (Jer 12:1). Jeremiah is not forgetting which of them is God and which is creature; still, he feels justified—compelled, even—to speak frankly to his Lord about what bothers him. If we are hesitant about speaking boldly to God, we could memorize Jeremiah's words and use them as a preface to our own.

The anonymous Canaanite woman of the Gospels who wants Jesus to cure her daughter is as fearless as Jeremiah and as persistent as Abraham. Between the accounts in Mark (7:24-30) and Matthew (15:21-28), we know that Jesus really wants to be alone, and the disciples clearly want to get rid of this woman. But she persists and Jesus listens. Their conversation is really an argument, one which she eventually wins. It is almost impossible to imagine Jesus without a smile (Could one be bold and say a "grin"?) on his face as he finally yields to her: "For such a reply, be off now! The demon has already left your daughter."

These people—and many others in the Scriptures—are reverent before the Lord and still free to be themselves. Like Moses, they speak to God "face to face as one person speaks to another" (Ex 33:11).

The God we pray to is the same God who accepted the praising, the nagging, the scolding, and the pleading of our spiritual ancestors. Since God is "the same yesterday, today, and forever," perhaps we too could be more straight-forward and direct in our prayers. In fact, we might just as well be candid, since we know from many of the psalms that God is fully aware of what we are thinking anyway:

> Would not God have discovered this?
> For he knows the secrets of the heart (Ps 44:22).

For Discussion

1. Jesus tells us how loving and caring our Father is (Matt 7:11), and tells us to pray to him (Matt 6:5-14). How does a child speak to a loving parent? What does this teach us about the way to speak to our heavenly Parent?

2. In chapter 12 of Matthew's Gospel (v. 12), Jesus says how "precious a human being is," and in vv. 18-21 Matthew quotes Isaiah regarding the gentleness and mercy of God's servant Jesus. What do we learn from this about how approachable Jesus is and how he feels about us? How should this affect the way we pray?

3. Read and discuss Psalm 26 and the first five verses of Psalm 17, where the psalmist protests his innocence. Compare this with the words of the Pharisee in the temple (Luke 18:9-14). What is the difference? How do we strike a balance?

4. Discuss the possibility of learning by heart the words of Jeremiah (Jer 12:1). How would they work as a preface to prayer? Would they lead to direct conversation instead of memorized formulas? Try it and see.

5. In Psalm 86:17, the psalmist boldly asks God to grant him a "proof" of his favor. Yet many times in the Gospels, Jesus is angered by people who ask for a sign, a "proof." What is the difference? Why is this one acceptable and another—e.g. John 6:30—not?

6. Read the first six verses of Psalm 139: God "understands my thoughts from afar" and knows what I am thinking "even before a word is on my lips." Discuss this passage as it relates to being open and frank in our prayers.

7. In his letter to the Ephesians, Paul writes, "In Christ and through faith in him we can speak freely to God, drawing near him with confidence" (3:12). Decide what the passage means and how we can learn to do this.

8. Look again at the stories of Abraham and of the Canaanite woman, both very bold with God and both accepted by God. What can we learn from observing them?

2

Worthy of Trust

It was a tragic story. The man had been decent
and honest all his life, and yet suddenly people
turned against him without cause and made plans
to trap and destroy him. He was the kind of friend
who, when people were ill, had fasted and prayed
for them just as if they were his own family. But
when he was stricken, they gathered together and
laughed. Worse yet, they accused him of having
done evil things he had never even heard of, and
they found witnesses who swore, "We saw him
with our own eyes." After spreading vicious lies
about him, they laughed at his misfortune. At
times his faith faltered and he wondered why God
did not help him. In the end, however, he trusted,
sure that he would be freed from this injustice
and relieved of his anger and frustration. Confident of God's eventual help, he promised, "Then
my tongue shall recount your justice, your praise
all the day."

The victim—and hero—of this story is the speaker in Psalm 35. He sets us a good example of trusting in God's word even when things are at their worst and there seems to be no way out. Indeed, his temporary doubt is itself a comfort to us —we know what it is to have doubts. But always he chooses again to trust. Trust is another of those underlying attitudes of prayer in the psalms which we need in our own prayers.

We see trust here not as a synonym for faith, but rather as that aspect of faith which means confidence, a child-like certainty that God can and will do what he has said he would.

The psalmist has this kind of confidence. Throughout the psalms, we see him both preaching it and practicing it. "Many are the sorrows of the wicked," he tells us, "but kindness surrounds him who trusts in the Lord" (Ps 32:10). In this passage he appears to be calling "wicked" those who do *not* trust in the Lord, a strong statement indeed. In Psalm 37 we are advised in several ways to put our cares in God's hands and trust him completely:

> Trust in the Lord and do good,
>> that you may dwell in the land and enjoy
>> security (v. 3).

> Commit to the Lord your way;
>> trust in him, and he will act (v. 5).

> Leave it to the Lord, and wait for him (v. 7).

Psalm 112 assures us that the just person can be confident even in the face of bad news:

> An evil report he shall not fear;
>> his heart is firm, trusting in the Lord (v. 7).

The hearts of those who trust are so firm and unwavering, in fact, they are like Mt. Zion itself, "which is immovable; which forever stands" (Ps 125:1).

Besides preaching trust in these ways, and praising it, the psalmist tells us that he himself is a person of trust and that in the trials of daily life, trust bears him up. In other words, he practices what he preaches. For example, he can sleep well because of trust. Our friend the psalmist claims,

> As soon as I lie down, I fall peacefully asleep,
>> for you alone, O Lord,
>> bring security to my dwelling (Ps 4:9).

Which of us cannot recognize the truth of what he says about sleeping well? Remembering our own sleepless nights in times of anxiety, we might agree that a real test of trust in God's promises is whether we toss and turn or sleep peacefully. In another place he says,

> When I lie down in sleep,
>> I wake again, for the Lord sustains me (Ps 3:6).

He advises us to have this same peaceful confidence and tells us how useless it is to spend restless nights in worry:

> It is vain for you to rise early,
>> or put off your rest,

> You that eat hard-earned bread,
>> for he gives to his beloved in sleep (Ps 127:2).

What a marvelous comfort to know that God cares for us and provides for us even while we sleep. We can safely leave our cares to him.

Lest we lose heart comparing our inadequate trust to the psalmist's unquestioning faith, we might look at Psalm 6, where he admits that he too has had bad nights in spite of everything:

> I am wearied with sighing;
>> every night I flood my bed with weeping;
>> I drench my couch with my tears (v. 7).

Such an admission in no way cancels out what he says in other places about trust; it means only that like the rest of us sinners—we who eat hard-earned bread—he too has moments of failure. Despite those slips, though, his heart is still fixed on God: "In him my heart trusts, and I find help" (Ps 28:7).

The psalmist suggests a good device for dealing with doubts, one which worked for him and could work for us too. In Psalm 143 he is clearly at low ebb—"my spirit fails me"—and to restore this failing spirit, he recalls the past when God pulled him through dark times:

> I remember the days of old;
>> I meditate on all your doings,
>> the works of your hands I ponder (v. 5).

Surely we too could shore up our failing trust by recalling those times in our lives when God saved us from trouble and set us in a firm place.

There are times when enemies assail his trust, saying they can do all the evil they want and God does not see or punish them. But the psalmist calmly turns to the Lord and asserts that they are wrong:

> You do see, for you behold misery and sorrow,
>   taking them in your hands (Ps 10:14).

Trusting in the Lord and his promises would be a simple matter if there were no waiting involved, but the psalms reiterate what we know from our experience: our trust is tested by our having to wait. As we was in Psalm 37, we leave our needs to the Lord and then "we wait for him." But we are assured that our waiting will be rewarded; the psalmist encourages us: "No one who waits for [God] shall be put to shame." It is those who "heedlessly break faith"—that is, those who do not trust—who shall be disappointed (Ps 25:3). Like our own sometimes does, his waiting seems endless—"for you I wait all the day." It is also intense, for he likens it to the anxious longing of people on night watch·

> I trust in the Lord;
>   my soul trusts in his word.
> My soul waits for the Lord
>   more than sentinels wait for the dawn.

> (Ps 130:5-6)

During these times of waiting, sometimes all we can do is cling to the Lord's promises as the psalmist does and keep reminding ourselves over and over again, "The promises of the Lord are sure!" "The promises of the Lord are fire-tried!" (Pss 12:7; 18:31).

Abraham, like the psalmist, clung to such promises through sharp disappointments and long delays—and through the ultimate test when he was asked to sacrifice his son Isaac (Gen 22). Moses too endured periods of severe testing and waiting, but the writer of Hebrews tells us that Moses kept on trusting: "he persevered as if he were looking on the invisible God" (Heb 11:27). What a powerful picture these words create: to move through life's difficulties with the same confidence we would have if we were watching Jesus walking right alongside us and could reach out and touch him. The psalmist had seen the Lord this way with the eyes of faith: "I set the Lord ever before me; with him at my right hand, I shall not be disturbed" (Ps 16:8).

Reading the Gospels, we get the impression that Jesus wants us to trust him in precisely this way, but it seems that many of us are afraid to take him at his word. We appear to be afraid of "presuming" on God or of trusting too much. Yet in reading the Gospel accounts of Jesus' dealing with people, we would be hard pressed to find a passage where he chides anyone for trusting too much or for being presumptuous. We find just the opposite. In scene after scene we hear him voice sadness and disappointment when people do not trust enough.

A reading of just a few chapters of Matthew, for example, shows Jesus voicing both sadness and disappointment as he works among the people. To Peter after his attempt to walk on the water, Jesus says: "How little faith you have! Why did you falter?" (14:31). To his disciples when they misunderstand what he says about the leaven of the Pharisees: "How weak your faith is! Do you still not understand?" (16:8-9). To the people surrounding the possessed boy, he says: "What an unbelieving and perverse lot you are! How long must I remain with you? How long can I endure you?" (17:17). And to the disciples, when they ask why they could not drive the demon out: "Because you have so little trust" (17:20).

But with what pleasure Jesus responds when he meets a real believer. To the Canaanite woman, he says: "Woman, you have great faith! Your wish will come to pass" (15:28). To the centurion: "Go home. It shall be done because you trusted" (8:13). And to the woman with the hemorrhage: "Courage, daughter! Your faith has restored you to health" (9:22).

In fact, in one sentence Jesus sums up "all the law and the prophets" on the subject of trusting him, when he speaks to the people who come to tell him the daughter of Jairus is dead. He says simply, "Fear is useless. What is needed is trust" (Mark 5:36).

For Discussion

1. In Psalm 56:3-4, the psalmist says, "O Most High, when I begin to fear, in you will I trust." This sounds like a deliberate decision, a choice made after the fear had started moving in. Discuss how a person might *choose* to trust in times of trouble.

2. Psalm 18:31 says, "The promise of the Lord is fire-tried." In our lives, have we fire-tried God's promises? What are some of the Lord's promises? How can we try them?

3. The psalmist prays, "I bring my plea *expectantly*" (Ps 5:4). Jesus echoes this in Mark 11:24

where he says we must be "ready to believe" when we pray. Discuss the importance of expectant prayer. How can we be ready to believe?

4. There are two places in Joshua where we read of having to trust a promise:

In Joshua 6:2: The Lord says, "I *have delivered* Jericho and its king into your power." This uses the past tense, yet the people had to march around the city for six days and only on the seventh finally see the victory.

In Joshua 10:8: The Lord says to Joshua, "Do not fear them for I *have delivered* them into your power." Again, past tense, and yet the battle did not take place until after an all-night march. This is similar to the psalmist's statement, "The Lord will complete what he has done for me" (Ps 138:8). Discuss the trust that accepts the Lord's promise as kept even when the final results are not yet visible.

5. In another passage from Joshua (3:13), the priests carrying the ark of the covenant are told they should walk right into the Jordan River, and "when the soles of the feet of the

priest carrying the ark . . . touch the water of the Jordan, it will cease to flow." Notice, they cannot wait on the shore for the water to recede, but must get their feet wet—*then* the water will stop. This took real trust that God would keep his promise. And he did: the waters stopped. Have you ever had to step out **and get your feet wet**, going only on faith in God's promise? **Reflect** on what happened, and how it **might help deepen** your trust for the next test.

6. What are some ways we might learn to imitate the confidence of Moses and trust as if we too were "looking on the invisible God"?

7. "Everything is possible to one who trusts" (Mark 9:23). Do we really believe that?

3

Always and Everywhere

The old catechisms taught us about the four kinds of prayer: praise, thanksgiving, sorrow for sin, and petition. It was always made clear that although all prayer was good, of course, the highest and best was praise and adoration.

Few of us needed to be told what petitions were—we certainly knew how to ask for things—and we were reminded frequently to say "Thank you" when those petitions had been granted. We knew too, at least from the Act of Contrition, what reparation and sorrow for sin were. But when it came to praise, that noblest prayer of all, we fell short. In our personal prayer, we hardly used it at all unless we read it from a prayer book. Praising God was taken care of at Mass in the Gloria or the

Holy, Holy, Holy. Praying "Glory be to the Father" was as close as we came to personal praise.

For many people the situation has not changed even now that we are adults praying in our own words. "Please," and "Thank you," and "I'm sorry" come to our minds and lips quite naturally. But praise? That's a different story.

Looking again at the psalms, those prayers which are the handiwork of God himself, how different it is! There also we find petition, thanks, and repentance, but more than anything else, we find praise. The psalmist praises God in every imaginable situation, from moments of splendid joy to moments of desperate pain and fear. Always there is praise.

Sometimes it is difficult to separate praise and thanks in the psalms, as it is elsewhere. After all, when we thank God, we are praising him as well, and when we praise him for something he has *done* for us, such praise is indistinguishable from thanks. We might look at both praise and thanksgiving as having three levels. I praise God for what he *is*, for what he has *done*, for what he has done for *me*. I thank God for what he *is*, for what he has *done*, for what he as done for *me*. The purest, most unselfish of these prayers simply praises God for himself. In this prayer, we delight or stand in awe of who and what God is, for what we know of him and for what still remains mystery. Then we praise him for his mighty works, the magnificence of creation we see all around us, and last, we praise him for his specific kindness to us.

All these levels of praise are found in the psalms, prayers which we can use as our own just as they stand, or which we can use as models of praying in our own words. They show us the way.

Frequently we see the psalmist praising and thanking God for specific favors received. Praise pours forth because God has saved him from his enemies (Pss 9:4; 18:48-9), heard the sound of his pleading (Ps 28:6), and pulled him out of the pit of destruction and set him on solid ground (Ps 40:3). God has healed him and saved him from death (Ps 30:3-4). God is praised too for building up strength in the psalmist (Ps 138:3) and delivering him from all his fears. The psalmist responds to God's kindness in prayers of praise and invites his friends to join in.

We might ask ourselves whether we are as spontaneous and whole-hearted as the psalmist in making the praise of God our first response when we have been healed, reconciled with an enemy, or relieved of some fear.

The psalmist does not limit his praises only to those favors he has received for himself, however; he includes the wider blessings God has poured out on the whole community, the psalmist's people.

Psalm 147 is one of those which lists many good things God has done for Jerusalem, including blessing its children and giving it food, safety, and peace (vv. 12ff). Psalm 44 praises the victories God won for Israel in the past, and Psalm 107 lists a whole series of episodes, each telling of some powerful way God intervened to save his people: he led them forth from the wilderness, freed them from chains, cured their illness, saved them from the stormy sea, provided water in the desert. After each episode the psalmist offers "thanks to the Lord for his kindness."

The psalms have much to teach us about being equally sensitive in our prayers, observant of what "wondrous deeds" God has done for our households, our communities, our country. Do we see God's kindness in the good news in the home-town paper, the letter from a friend, or the phone call that puts our mind at ease?

Sometimes forgetting personal needs completely, the psalmist breaks into praise of God simply for what he is, for what the psalmist has experienced of the Lord's divine qualities. God's justice, for example, is highly praised (Pss 7:18; 9:12, 15). So are his kindness and faithfulness (Pss 31:22; 108:4-5). Which of us cannot share the psalmist's wonder at God's power displayed in a mighty storm, where the "God of glory thunders" and "the voice of the Lord strikes fiery flames"? (Ps 29). Psalm 65 is another which glorifies God for the marvels of his creation, for watering the land and blanketing it with grain, for providing abundant flocks and lush harvests. Even the fields and valleys "shout and sing for joy."

At times this generous God strikes the psalmist

as being so mysterious that it is nearly impossible to find words to praise him: "His greatness is unsearchable" (Ps 145:3). All of Psalm 139 marvels at the endless wonders of God, including the marvel of how each of us is "fearfully, wonderfully made." We could meditate for hours on these very wonders—and indeed some doting parents do just that when there is a new baby in the house.

One phrase which recurs regularly throughout the psalms as a unique form of praise is "for your name's sake." This phrase is usually attached to some favor the psalmist is requesting or anticipating, as in "He leads me in right paths for his name's sake" (Ps 23:3). What does it mean to ask God to do something for *us*, but for *his* name's sake? Ordinarily when we speak of doing something for someone's sake, we mean to do it for that person's benefit or advantage—"I kept the secret for my friend's sake." Perhaps it seems far-fetched to think we could do anything for God's advantage or benefit, but the psalmist has no doubts about what to do for the sake of God's name: he offers praise. To ask God to do something for "his name's sake," then, means to request a favor, the granting of which will bring praise and glory to his name. His goodness to us gives glory to him.

Such a prayer can be a kind of promise to God as well as a reminder to the one who prays. When Psalm 109 prays, "Lord, deal kindly with me for your name's sake," the psalmist is saying in a sense, "Lord, if you deal kindly with me, it will give glory to your name; your kindness to me will glorify you." Such a prayer also reminds the one praying not to forget that it was God who showed the kindness and whose name thus deserves the praise and thanks.

The psalmist uses this phrase of praise for a variety of things: "preserve me," "lead and guide me," "pardon my guilt," "pardon our offenses," "guide me on right paths"—all "for your name's sake, O Lord." It is a phrase—composed by the Holy Spirit, remember—which we may well incorporate into our own prayer requests, so that our petitions are never separated from praise and thanks: "For your name's sake bring reconciliation to our family. For your name's sake, help me through this difficult time. For your name's sake, help me overcome this sin in my life." Perhaps in time we will get even bolder and like the psalmist will say not, "Help me for your name's sake," but rather, "You *will* help me for your name's sake"!

Daily the Church prays in the preface of the Mass, "Lord we do well always and everywhere to give you thanks." Since thanks and praise are virtually interchangeable, we can pray with equal truth, "We do well always and everywhere to give you praise." If we take such a prayer at face value, we are saying there is no time or situation in our lives in which we cannot praise and thank God—quite a revolutionary thought when we consider some of the stickier, even painful and dangerous, predicaments of our lives. Would we really "do well" to praise God in the midst of those?

The psalmist does just that. We find the psalms praising not only when there has been victory, or rescue, or healing, but also when there is suffering and dire need. Even psalms that begin as complaints or cries of distress include some praise. In Psalm 69, called "A Cry of Anguish in Great Distress," the psalmist is "afflicted and in pain," yet exclaims, "I will praise the name of the Lord in song, and I will glorify him with thanksgiving" (v. 31). This is a tough model to follow, but it is one we see frequently in the psalms: praise in the midst of trouble. Psalm 42 is a good illustration of the kind of interior conversation we all have had with ourselves when we are in such distress. The psalmist observes himself downcast, in mourning, oppressed by an enemy, but he turns and talks to himself, trying to build himself up: "Hope in God! For I shall again be thanking him, in the presence of my Savior and my God." This is like saying to ourselves, "Yes, things are miserable today; I am worried and afraid, but cheer up! I know that soon again I will be thanking and praising God for having helped me through this and made it all come out right—even better than I dare now hope."

Past generations of school children learned that the answer to the question, "Why did God make us?" was "God made us to know, love, and serve him in this world and to be happy with him forever in the next." More recent students have learned a new version of the answer: "God made us to show forth his goodness and to share with us his everlasting happiness in heaven." If St. Paul were to prepare that particular religion lesson, however, he might state the answer as he did in the letter to the Ephesians. Three times in the first chapter, Paul makes it clear that God made us to praise him. We are "a people God made his own to praise his glory," Paul says; God "predestined us to praise his glory" and to "praise the glorious favor he has bestowed on us" in Jesus.

Actually the answers come out the same, for to "know, love, and serve God" *is* to praise him. It is *because* he shows forth his goodness that we praise him, and it is in praising that we share his everlasting happiness in heaven. Clearly we are meant to be a people of praise!

For Discussion

1. We have heard a lot about how God desires praise, but we live in a consumer oriented society and we might find ourselves asking, "What do we get out of praise?" Check the following passages for a partial answer: 2 Chronicles 29:30; Ps 50:14-15; Ps 18:4.

2. See verses 14 and 23 of Psalm 50. What is a "sacrifice of praise"? Could it mean praising God even during times when it is difficult, a sacrifice, to do so? Why would such praise especially "glorify" God as it says in v. 23?

3. In Psalm 66:17, the psalmist says, "When I appealed to God in words, praise was on the tip of my tongue." What do you think this means? Relate this to Paul's statement that our petitions should be full of gratitude (Phil 4:6).

37

4. Why is praise considered the highest form of prayer?

5. Discuss these comments about David: "With his every deed he offered thanks to God most high, in words of praise. With his whole being he loved his Maker and daily had his praises sung" (Sir 47:8). Verse 11 of that chapter tells how God responded to David's praise. (Remember David was a sinner.) How can we offer praise and thanks to God with our "every deed"?

6. See Sirach 43:29-34. Reflect on ways we might praise God for what we do *not* know about him as well as for what we do know.

7. Spend some time reflecting on how "fearfully, wonderfully made" you are (Ps 139:14). Praise God for it. Think of someone you have a hard time loving and reflect on how "fearfully, wonderfully made" that person is. Can you praise God for that too?

8. In Psalm 147:12ff the psalmist lists many reasons to give praise to God. Could you—either alone or as a group—re-write this with your own reasons for praise?

4

Hard Time

Once we found great comfort in praying, but now it is a chore; once God seemed so close we could almost reach out and touch him, but now he seems nowhere in sight; once Mass and the sacraments were sources of joy and comfort, but now we go only out of duty; once we looked forward eagerly to that daily quiet time of reading and reflecting and praying, but now we can scarcely force ourselves to sit down and take the time at all. We have become clock watchers. What in the world happened? What went wrong? Why this drought?

When a man is sentenced and sent to prison, we say he is "doing time." And when an inmate doing time hits a low period, a period of depression, hopelessness, and despair, his fellow prisoners nod sympathetically and say he is doing "hard time." We might find that expression useful for describing those experiences in our lives when prayer is hard, dry, and apparently profitless. We are doing "hard time," an earthy way to express spiritual dryness. St. John of the Cross uses a more exalted term, "the dark night of the soul." While most of us might be hesitant to apply that to ourselves and would be more comfortable speaking of doing "hard time," nevertheless we all have felt in our own small way what it means to have our well run dry. How in the world do we cope with this awful barren dryness?

First of all we need to know that if we have been faithful to our commitment to pray and read and listen, and still we find no comfort or satisfaction in it, then what we are experiencing is normal and may, in fact, be a gift from God.

Whatever we choose to call it—dryness or darkness or hard time—we need to know that this time will come periodically throughout our lives. We find assurance of this in the psalms as well as other places in Scripture: God's followers do experience times when he seems to have abandoned them. Knowing this, we will not lose hope or drop our practice of prayer and Scripture reading when it happens to us.

Looking at the psalms, we discover several images used to convey this feeling that God no longer sees or hears us. One is the idea that God is "hiding his face." We know how children behave when their mother hides her face behind her hands: they are disturbed and will try to pull her hands away. This is how the psalmist feels.

In Psalm 13 he asks, "How long will you hide your face from me?" (v. 2). Sometimes as in Psalm 27, it becomes a plea: "You my glance seeks. . . . Hide not your face from me" (vv. 8-9). He is in real distress in Psalm 31: "Once I said in my anguish, 'I am cut off from your sight'" (v. 23). These moments of desolation feel endless, for the psalmist says, "My eyes have failed with looking for my God," and "How long, O Lord? Will you hide yourself forever?" (Pss 69:4; 89:47). Pleading for God to reveal himself, the psalmist prays, "Hide not your face from me, lest I become like those who go down into the pit" (143:7). Could we not agree with the psalmist that the feeling that God is hiding his face from us really is the *pits?*

Another way in which the psalmist expresses this desolate feeling is that God has removed himself completely and forgotten him. "Why, O Lord, do you stand aloof?" (Ps 10:1). "How long, O Lord? Will you utterly forget me?" (13:2). In another place, the psalmist is very bold, arguing with God:

> "Why do you forget me?
> Why must I go about in mourning,
>   with the enemy oppressing me?"
> It crushes my bones that my foes mock me,
>   as they say to me day after day,
>   "Where is your God?" (Ps 42:10-11).

A third way in which spiritual dryness is expressed in the psalms is, appropriately enough, with the image of thirst:

O God, you are my God whom I seek;
for you my flesh pines and my soul thirsts
like the earth parched, lifeless and without water.
(Ps 63:2. See also Ps 42)

The psalms, then, provide ample evidence this feeling that God has abandoned us is normal and to be expected. But we find something else too: this absence is for a time only, and even "in the pits" the psalmist is certain of God's return in his own good time. We need to be aware of this when our wells have run dry and we are thirsty. These psalms are our prayers too, and because they are divinely inspired, we can look to them for help and comfort.

Psalm 30 tells the whole story very well: "God's anger lasts but a moment: a lifetime his good will. At nightfall weeping enters in"—that's the dry time—"But with the dawn, rejoicing." It ends on an exultant note which should encourage us:

You changed my mourning into dancing;
you took off my sackcloth and clothed me with
gladness (v. 12).

We might also look to Psalm 27 for encouragement. It too begins with the psalmist doing hard time: "Hide not your face from me; do not in anger repel your servant" (v. 9). But the closing lines reveal confidence that God will show his face again: "I believe that I shall see the bounty of the Lord in the land of the living." (That means here and now, a cheering thought.) "Wait for the Lord with courage; be stouthearted, and wait for the Lord" (vv. 13-14). A striking passage in Isaiah also tells both the beginning and the ending of the hard-times story:

> For a brief moment, I abandoned you,
>   but with great tenderness I will take you back.
> In an outburst of wrath, for a moment
>   I hid my face from you;
> But with enduring love, I take pity on you,
>   says the Lord, your redeemer (54:7-9).

We know of course that God does not really abandon us in an outburst of wrath, but it could very well appear that way to one whose prayer life has suddenly gone empty, whose spirit is "dry, lifeless, and without water." The psalmist does not sugarcoat it; rather, he admits it is tough to wait for the Lord in hard times; it takes courage, he says, and a stout heart.

There are heartening words in the book of Lamentations where the speaker, sounding very much like us when we are doing hard time, says to God, "You wrapped yourself in a cloud which prayer could not pierce" (3:44). But see what else is there: "Good is the Lord to one who waits for him, to the soul that seeks him. It is good to hope in silence for the saving help of the Lord" (3:25-26).

This leads us to the most important thing we need to know about these lean times: they are for a purpose; they are good for us; they accomplish something in us. Not only do we have the comfort of knowing that they are normal and will pass, but we also have the reassurance that they will bear fruit—provided we are faithful. They will teach us how close God really is.

We get some good advice from Psalm 37: "Wait for the Lord and keep his way." (That is, stay faithful to prayer even when it is hard going.) "He will promote you to ownership of the land" (v. 34). This "land" probably refers to heaven, but it would be apt also to envision it as experiencing again the comforts of the Lord's presence when the hard times have passed.

So we struggle along, putting in our prayer time daily, reading the Bible, waiting, and hoping it's true that "the Lord is close to the broken-hearted and those who are crushed in spirit he saves" (Ps 34:19). We fight the temptation to rake the yard or make an urgent phone call instead; we keep pulling our meandering thoughts back to our prayer and try to mean it as we pray with the psalmist, "It is good for me that I have been afflicted, that I may learn your statutes. . . . In your faithfulness you have afflicted me" (Ps 119:71, 75). But we feel like a motor desperately in need of oil—no wonder these times are called "dry."

When God "shows his face" again, we may have learned the truth of what Psalm 25 tells us: "All the paths of the Lord are kindness and constancy toward those who keep his covenant and his decrees" (v. 10). If we have been faithful to prayer through the difficulty, we should experience the good results; we will see that all the paths of the Lord *are* kindness, even those that had looked bare and rocky. It is reminiscent of another comforting line from Scripture: "All things work together for good to those that love God" (Rom 8:28).

If these dry times are supposed to accomplish good results, what might those be?

First, dry times can teach us our own helplessness. When prayer is a joy and all our spiritual practices are smooth and delightful, it is easy for us to get the impression that we are doing something and achieving growth on our own. Suddenly, even though we are doing everything the same, we get no comfort at all. We become aware that all is God's doing, and there is nothing we can do on our own. We learn to depend completely on God's mercy, and we say with Isaiah, "Lord, it is you who have accomplished all we have done" (26:12). Instead of walking by feeling or emotion, we walk in the dark—that is, by faith—and our faith is deepened.

Second, the dry times accepted faithfully can be times of eliminating some sin or sinful tendencies from our lives, perhaps those we have been least aware of. Psalm 19 asks, "Who can detect failings? Cleanse me from my unknown faults" (v. 13). Psalm 90 also speaks of our "hidden sins" which God keeps in his "scrutiny" (v. 8). These can be purged away if we humbly and patiently struggle through the dry times and live by faith.

Third, if we show constancy even when prayer is very difficult, we can be sure there is growth occurring where we cannot see it right away. Belief in this truth keeps us going. We think of the natural phenomenon of a dry, barren, desert area. It appears all bleak and arrid, yet scientists tell us that deep underneath, many feet down, there runs a steady stream of clear, cold water. We have to trust that no matter how dry and barren our prayer life appears to be, God is working in us down deep, like that clear running water.

Writing about a time when he was critically ill and had discontinued all pain killing medication to begin a new approach to his disease, Norman Cousins observed, "I could stand the pain as long as I knew progress was being made."[1] This could be said of our hard times too: we can stand the "pain" as long as we know progress is being made. This could be our prayer: "Lord, I accept this dry, thirsty time, but please do not let it be wasted. Work in me, Lord, way down deep, and change me according to your will." It is helpful during a period like this, when God is hiding his face from us, to simply *choose* to trust, to make conscious, explicit decisions to believe: "Lord, I choose to trust you even though I do not feel it at all."

If we remain faithful during hard times, they will bring some growth: purer faith, deeper prayer, greater love, more patience, or calmer

---

1. Norman Cousins, *Anatomy of an Illness* (New York: W. W. Norton and Company, 1979) 38.

dependence on God. God does not prune and trim needlessly—there will be growth: like Ezekiel's dry bones, we will come to life again.

Probably no one says it better than Isaiah. He includes the hunger and the thirst; then he describes the closeness of God when the hard time has been accomplished, the sentence served:

> The Lord will give the bread you need
>   and the water for which you thirst.
> No longer will your Teacher hide himself,
>   but with your own eyes you shall see your
>   Teacher,
> While from behind, a voice shall sound in your
>   ears:
>   This is the way: walk in it (Is 30:20).

For Discussion

1. Read Mark 16:9-20, where he describes the disciples' situation during the time between the
   crucifixion and the resurrection: they were
   "grieving and weeping." Jesus "took them to
   task for their disbelief and stubbornness."
   Discuss this episode as it relates to the idea of
   "hard time" in prayer.

2. How might keeping a prayer journal help a person through times when prayer is hard?

3. Reflect on and discuss the following words of
   Jesus: "I am the true vine and my Father is the
   vinegrower. He prunes away every barren
   branch, but the fruitful ones he trims clean to
   increase their yield" (John 15:1-2).

4. Jesus said to Thomas, "Blest are they who have
   not seen and have believed" (John 20:29). How

48

might this be a consoling prayer for us when prayer is hard and we do not "see"?

5. Jesus told his disciples, "A little while and you will see me no more; again a little while, and you will see me" (John 16:16 RSV/CE). One writer comments that in the original Greek text, the first word for "seeing" meant physical vision, and the other meant spiritual vision. So the passage could be paraphrased thus: "A little while and you will no longer see me physically, and again a little while you will see me spiritually."[2] How could we apply this to those times when God seems to hide his face from us?

6. One of the things we learn in dry times of prayer is that we must depend on God, not on ourselves, for spiritual growth. In this connection, discuss 2 Cor 3:5 and John 3:27. What are some of the wrong-headed attitudes we have about "earning" our own salvation?

7. Think about this principle of the spiritual life: "Do not forget in the dark what you have learned in the light." Discuss it in connection with "hard time" in prayer.

2. John C. H. Wu, *The Interior Carmel* (New York: Sheed and Ward, 1953) 171. 2.

5

Into the Temple

The more we pray the psalms, the more easily we can believe their divine authorship. The increasing depth of our understanding—of God's power, of his tenderness, and especially, of his very being—each time we read the psalms, indicates a divine author. But the humanity of the author comes through clearly too: enmeshed with the profound words of praise and love, we see the speaker's anger and rage, his hatred for enemies, his fear and discouragement, his disgust with his sins. Whatever other unattractive qualities he may reveal about himself, however, there is one thing we will never hear the psalmist say: "Well, today is the sabbath, so I suppose I will have to go to the Temple. I just don't seem to get anything out of it anymore." At no time does he drag his feet or have to be convinced to go to the Temple and pray; it is not mere duty. He exclaims, "I *rejoiced* because they said to me, 'We will go up to the house of the Lord'" (Ps 122:1). Clearly he loves the Temple, the "tenting place" of God's glory. It is the center of his world, the place where God dwells.

When the psalmist is away from Jerusalem, he longs for the Temple and dreams nostalgically of the good old days when he "went with the throng and led them in procession to the house of God, amid loud cries of joy and thanksgiving" (Ps 42:5). So precious to him is God's house that he would rather lie on its doorstep than stay in the houses of the wicked; he would trade a thousand days anywhere else to one day in the house of God (Ps 84:11).

Imagine the astonishment of the psalmist if he had learned that the day was coming when God's friends would never have to be away from the Temple, would never again have to yearn for it from a distance, but would have it always with them—indeed, they would themselves *be* the temple! This is exactly what Jesus revealed when he spoke to his followers at the Last Supper: "Anyone who loves me will be true to my word, and my Father will love him; we will come to him and make our dwelling place with him" (John 14:23). In promising the strength and comfort of the Holy Spirit after his departure, Jesus said that "he remains with you and will be within you" (John 14:17).

Paul is just as explicit in his letter to the Corinthians. "Are you not aware," he asks them, "that you are the temple of God, and that the Spirit of God dwells in you? . . . For the temple of God is holy, and you are that temple" (1 Cor 3:16-17). He reiterates in chapter 6: "You must know that your body is the temple of the Holy Spirit who is within . . ." (v. 19).

This revelation greatly enriches the way we pray the psalms—or any other prayers, for that matter. Whereas the psalmist longed for the Temple in Jerusalem, recalling its beauty and the loveliness of God's presence there, we can look within ourselves and "gaze on the loveliness of the Lord and contemplate his temple" right where we are. The psalmist's references to God's house—his temple, court, dwelling place, or tent—all come to mean his very presence with us and within us here and now.

When we pray the psalms and come to these "house of the Lord" passages, we think not of the great Temple in Jerusalem, or of a church, or even of God in heaven; we think of God in *us.* Also when we take this attitude of the psalmist and apply it in our other prayer, we remember God is not confined to a tabernacle or church, but is in ourselves and our sisters and brothers. How heartily we can join the psalmist, then, when he prays, "One thing I ask of the Lord; this I seek: To dwell in the house of the Lord all the days of my life," for it means that we too want God close to us all our days; we want to dwell in his presence so that we will experience his goodness and kindness all the days of our lives (Ps 27:4).

Thinking of God being in the inner temple rather than being restricted to any one place can lead to some intriguing insights. Think of mobility for one thing. The great Temple loved by the psalmist stood solidly in the holiest part of Jerusalem, but our temple, our "holy of holies," goes wherever we go. It is like the ark of the covenant which traveled with God's people in the wilderness, always indicating his presence among them. We are now the ark of God's covenant, taking the Lord with us on a family trip in the car, on a jet plane to the coast, on the bus to school, and on an outing to the company picnic. The ark accompanies the homemaker to the clothesline, the commuter on the daily train, and the firefighter on the big red truck. Joggers might be pleased to realize that on their early morning run they are living, breathing arks of the covenant doing a nine-minute mile.

Another quality our inner temple shares with the holy of holies of the psalmist is its mystery. The outermost limits of the Temple were public, open to all. Next came the Temple proper, with numerous courts built higher and more restricted as they progressed to the highest and most secret of all—the holy of holies. While the other parts of the Temple were busy and noisy, this place was silent, heavily draped, entered only by officiating priests at specified times. Most worshipers never saw it but held it in awe from afar as the most sacred of all places, the place where God was most powerfully present.

Are not our "temples" somewhat like this mysterious sanctuary? We have our public court, the face which is open to all, but we grow more private and mysterious as we get closer to our own innermost heart where the Spirit of God dwells. Who, after all, really knows the heart of another person? Like Paul we ask, "Who knows a person's innermost self but the person's own spirit within?" (1 Cor 2:11). Even between the closest of friends, the most intimate of lovers, even in this age of frankness and sharing, only God truly knows the holy of holies that is in each person. In this inner temple there is constant praying just as there was in Jerusalem's great Temple, for "the Spirit himself makes intercession for us with groanings that cannot be expressed in speech" (Rom 8:26).

Knowing that whatever the psalmist could do in his Temple, we can do in ours, gives special meaning to those "house of God" passages in the psalms. When the psalm says, "Happy they who dwell in your house! continually they praise you" (Ps 84:5), the words remind us to rejoice over God's nearness to *us*, to realize that we can praise him any time, any place—"always and everywhere." When the psalm exclaims, "O God, we ponder your kindness within your temple" (Ps 48:10), we can ponder too the immensity of God's kindness that he has "pitched his tent" within us. When the psalmist says to God, "I, because of your abundant kindness, will enter your house; I will worship at your holy temple" (Ps 5:8), we know we can do the very same thing by finding a quiet time and place daily and worshiping at the temple that we carry with us. When the psalm calls for the prayers of "those who stand in the house of the Lord during the hours of night" (Ps 134:1), we are reassured that the Comforter lives within us ready to pray with us and for us on sleepless nights. When the psalmist says he was in distress and called out to the Lord for help, and "from his temple he heard my voice, and my cry to him reached his ears" (Ps 18:7), we know we can reach the Lord for help any time too, calling out in our distress and need, confident that he hears even our unspoken prayers.

The rub, of course, is that I am not the only one with this inner temple; you have one, too, and so do all those who love God and keep his word (John 15:23). That changes things. We must show for all those mini-temples we meet the same reverence and respect the psalmist showed for the Temple—a far tougher kind of reverence than simply being quiet and respectful in church. One prayer which can be very helpful in heightening our awareness of God's presence is a simple line I read once in a letter from a missioner in Nepal: the Christians there greet each other by saying, "Praise to God who dwells within you." This

wonderfully versatile little prayer can make us
more keenly aware of God's presence in ourselves
("Praise to God who dwells within me.") as well as
in others. ("Praise to God who dwells within
them.") It can even be adapted easily to praying
for someone toward whom we are feeling anger
or animosity or simply used for intercession.
Prayed repeatedly like a Jesus prayer, it creates an
active link between God in us and God in the one
for whom we pray.

When the parish or community comes together for worship on the weekend, each person
comes as one of the many dwelling places of the
Lord. We bring all that has gone on that week in
our secret temples, the sacred places where God
has been praised, thanked, scolded, appealed to,
and relaxed with. Then, as we read in Ephesians,
together we "form a building . . . with Christ
Jesus himself as the capstone." Our slightly dusty,
rusty, musty temples are "fitted together and take
shape as a holy temple in the Lord; in him [we] are
being built into this temple, to become a dwelling
place for God in the Spirit" (Eph 2:20-22).

For Discussion

1. Reminisce a bit: how did you first learn about God and about prayer? Where did you picture God to be when you prayed? How has that changed over the years?

2. Reflect on the meaning of this statement by one of the saints: "God is more intimate to me than I am to myself." Is it possible for God to be closer to us than we are to ourselves? In what way?

3. "Draw close to God and he will draw close to you" (James 4:8). Think of all the ways that one might "draw close" to God. How does God "draw close" to us?

4. In 1 John 4:12 we read, "No one has ever seen God. Yet if we love one another God dwells in

us, and his love is brought to perfection in us."
Verse 16 adds, "God is love, and he who abides
in love abides in God, and God in him." Discuss
this connection between God in us and loving
our neighbor.

5. Discuss the possible uses and values of the
   prayer, "Praise to God who dwells within me
   . . . you . . . them. . . ."

6. In Psalm 42:3, the psalmist prays longingly,
   "When shall I go and behold the face of God?"
   The scripture notes tell us this was a Hebrew
   expression meaning, "When can I visit the
   Temple?" Read the first half of the psalm. How
   could a modern Christian read it to mean a
   desire to spend time daily quietly present to
   God in the inner temple?

7. Think about taking Jesus in our inner temple
   wherever we go: meetings, gatherings, work,
   recreation—everywhere. How might our con-
   sciously taking Jesus along change those ac-
   tivities?

8. What might we do to develop a keener awareness of God's dwelling within us?

9. Read and think about the following passage.
   What does it mean to you? "There is deep
   within us a place apart. Perhaps if we begin to

explore it we will discover we have made it into a bit of a storeroom. Perhaps it is even so crammed with junk we can hardly get in or close the door. Saint Benedict in his Rule reminds monks: 'The oratory should be what it is called—a place of prayer. Let nothing else be done or kept there.' We may have to do some housecleaning. But we do have this place within where we can at any moment retire, close the door (as our Lord said) and enjoy for that moment a place apart. Get to know that inner cell. You will come to love it and it will come to be a true friend. When you are harassed or weary you will begin to experience it reaching out to you, beckoning: Come apart and rest awhile. In its deep, cool darkness, sometimes illumined by a light not of our making, a moment can be a refreshing step into eternity, a coming home to the solitude of God."[1]

---

1. Basil M. Pennington, O.C.S.O., "A Place Apart," *Spiritual Life* 29, no. 2 (Summer 1983) 72.

6

The Enemy

The Book of Psalms is a "how-to" book: it teaches us to pray as the psalmist prays. We can confidently follow its instructions and appropriate the attitudes we find because they are the Lord's own prayers. Thus in the psalms we learn to speak to God frankly, openly, face to face. We learn to imitate the psalmist's attitudes of trust and praise. We learn too how to pray through the times when God seems to hide his face. We take the psalmist's songs of love for the Temple and use them to praise God's dwelling within each of his people. So far so good. But what are we to do when, praying the psalms, we suddenly come upon the psalmist addressing his enemies:

> Happy the man who shall repay you the evil you
> have done us!
> Happy the man who shall seize and smash
> your little ones against the rock! (Ps 137:8-9).

We shrink from the words or skip over them as if they were not there. If we choose to memorize a psalm, we certainly do not choose one that says we would like God to rain burning coals on our enemies' heads and cast them into the sea never to rise (Ps 140:11). Instead of turning aside from these passages as if God had made an embarrassing blunder, however, we can handle them honestly and even use them productively in our praying.

For one thing we need to recognize that although the writers of the Old Testament, including Psalms, were divinely inspired, their revelation was incomplete—like Paul's seeing "indistinctly, as in a mirror" (1 Cor 13:12). Only with the coming of Jesus did we see the light, the full revelation of God's plan and a new understanding of many Old Testament passages. Whereas the psalm asks God to break the teeth of the wicked and strike the enemies on the cheek (Ps 3:8), Jesus teaches us to love the wicked and to turn the other cheek (Matt 5:39). He makes the difference between old and new unmistakably clear: "You have heard the commandment, 'You shall love your countryman and hate your enemy.' My command to you is: love your enemies, pray for your persecutors" (Matt 5:43-44).

This leaves no doubt; we do not pray the "enemy" psalms from the same point of view the psalmist had, but we do not need to discard them either. There are ways of using them profitably.

When we pray, as in Psalm 35 for example, "Fight against those who fight against me; war against those who make war upon me," we can think of the enemies Paul speaks of in Ephesians: "Our battle is not against human forces but against the principalities and powers, the rulers of this world of darkness, the evil spirits in the regions above" (6:12). Against such enemies, we can feel perfectly comfortable hurling all the curses of the psalmist: may they be destroyed, cast into the pit, disgraced and shamed, dashed against the rocks, tossed like leaves in a whirlwind, chased over dark and slippery paths!

These forces of evil are the enemies Jesus overthrew by his death and resurrection. It was he who finally accomplished what the psalmist had prayed for: he routed the enemies and destroyed them. Colossians uses the same war-like language to describe this victory: "Thus did God disarm the principalities and the powers. He made a public show of them, and leading them off captive, triumphed in the person of Christ" (2:15). Just what the psalmist ordered.

A second way we can put the "enemy" psalms to good use in our prayers is by considering our sins as the enemy. The psalms give us ways to pray for God's strength against our own failures in following Jesus. When we pray the psalmist's words, "Rescue me from the clutches of my enemies and my persecutors" (Ps 31:16), we could mean "Rescue me from my sharp, critical tongue,"

"Rescue me from my small mindedness and envy," or "Rescue me from my pride." As we struggle to overcome some bad habit, we might pray against this enemy as the psalmist prays against his: "In your kindness destroy my enemies; bring to nought all my foes, for I am your servant" (Ps 143:12). Looking for guidance against some personal demon or vice, we pray with the psalmist, "Because of my enemies, guide me in your justice; make straight your way before me" (Ps 5:9). Whatever sin we want to eliminate from our lives, whatever hatred or prejudice or self-indulgence plagues us, we can heartily plead as the psalmist does: "Give me not up to the wishes of my foes" (Ps 27:12).

A careful reading of Psalms teaches us one particularly helpful lesson when it comes to coping with our own sinfulness. Notice how helpless the psalmist feels against his foes, how totally he depends on God, knowing it is impossible for him to rescue himself:

> Hearken, O God, to my prayer;
>   turn not away from my pleading;
>   give heed to me, and answer me.
> I rock with grief, and am troubled
>   at the voice of the enemy and the clamor of the
>   wicked (Ps 55:2-4).

In the same way, we recognize from sad experience that our best intentions and whipped-up will power are not enough to defeat sin in our lives. We need God's power against our enemies

just as the psalmist did. When at last he is saved
from the enemy, the psalmist knows that he has
not done it on his own, and he gives God the
credit:

> He rescued me from my mighty enemy
>> and from my foes, who were too powerful for
>> me.
> They attacked me in the day of my calamity,
>> but the Lord came to my support (Ps 18:18-19).

If only we could have that same certainty instead of becoming discouraged over our sins. The
psalmist says confidently, "All my enemies shall be
put to shame in utter terror; they shall fall back in
sudden shame" (Ps 6:11). The first few lines of
Psalm 27 show the same optimism. In fact while
still in the midst of the struggle, the psalmist
knows he can count on a happy ending, and so he
prays, "Even now my head is held high above my
enemies on every side" (Ps 27:6). Using that same
spirit of hope and trust, we need to pray for God's
help to overcome our frailties.

It is important though to keep a balance in this
matter. While we are praying for our sins to be
"cast into the pit" or "routed and destroyed," let us
remember to be gentle and not condemn ourselves along with our sins. Jesus gives us the
lesson by word and example to hate the sin while
loving the sinner, and we have to do that for ourselves as well as for others. Even with his incomplete vision, the psalmist knows why God
helps him against the enemy: "He set me free in

the open, and rescued me, *because he loves me"* (Ps 18:20). In fact, he can see that not surrendering to the enemy is the very test of God's love: "That you love me I know by this, that my enemy does not triumph over me" (Ps 41:12). Similarly, though we may have to battle our sins for a lifetime, we know we will not be overcome by them. God loves us too much for that.

Just as Jesus was gentle and forgiving with repentant sinners, so can we safely be gentle and forgiving with ourselves and our weakness. Taking a lesson from Paul, we never give in totally to discouragement because of our weakness. Rather, we remember what Jesus told him: "My grace is enough for you, for in weakness power reaches perfection" (2 Cor 12:9). As the psalmist prayed for the power of the Lord to save him, we too pray that the power of Christ will be with us and overcome our enemies. For one indication of how far God is willing to go for us in defeating our enemy, sin, we could ponder that extraordinary passage in Paul's letter to the Corinthians: "For our sakes God made him who did not know sin, to be sin, so that in him we might become the very holiness of God" (2 Cor 5:21).

For Discussion

1. Read again Paul's description of the enemies we fight against (Eph 6:12). Where do we see and how do we experience these "rulers of this world of darkness" in everyday life?

2. Paul writes, "In him who is the source of my strength I have strength for everything" (Phil 4:13). Who is that source? How do we tap that source for the strength to resist sin?

3. St. Augustine wrote, "We make a ladder of our vices, if we trample those same vices underfoot." What do you think he meant by this? What kind of ladder?

4. Looking again at the passages from Psalms quoted in this chapter, compare the psalmist's attitude towards enemies to that of Christ and his new commandment. Do we sometimes find

ourselves thinking more like the psalmist than like Jesus?

5. It can be very complicated and confusing to hate our sin, love ourselves, rejoice in our weakness and trust in God all at the same time. Read and discuss what Paul says about dealing with the same problem (Rom 7:14-25). What is his final answer? Compare it to the psalmist's answer: "That you love me I know by this, that my enemy does not triumph over me" (Ps 41:12).

6. "If anyone is in Christ, he is a new creation" (2 Cor 5:17). What does this mean? How does it enter into our comparison of the Old and the New Testament view of the enemy, sin?

7. Reflect on that dramatic statement of Paul's to the Corinthians. "For our sakes God made him who did not know sin to be sin, so that in him we might become the very holiness of God." What does it mean for us?

8. The psalmist asks God to dash his enemies against the rock. Thinking of our sins as the enemy, recall all the places where God is referred to as our Rock (e.g., Ps 18:2-3), or in the New Testament where Peter is the rock. In what sense can we think of dashing our sins against Jesus the Rock? Against the Church?

Notes